"What a wonderful idea to offer meditations aimed at our Enneagram types! Signature salve for signature sins. Juanita Rasmus is a friend and fellow One. I knew I felt we had much in common, and now I know why. Our DNA has burdened us both with reforming the world, which I've discovered comes with many more downs than ups. It was a pleasure to read Juanita's journey from control and frustration to acceptance, serenity, and playfulness."

Gary W. Moon, founding executive director of the Martin Institute and Dallas Willard Center, Westmont College, and author of *Becoming Dallas Willard*

"As a fellow Enneagram One, I found myself on almost every page of Juanita Campbell Rasmus's exploration of the problems and possibilities inherent in who we are. This little book offered me encouragement and comfort. Juanita's reflections issue an invitation to all Enneagram Ones to live with greater joy and freedom."

Amy Julia Becker, author of *White Picket Fences* and *A Good and Perfect Gift*

"I met Juanita Campbell Rasmus while she cofacilitated a men's spiritual retreat at the Center for Action and Contemplation. I walked into the session and was simply amazed by the presence of the Spirit in her. She's a One no doubt, but she's so much more!"

Richard Rohr, OFM, author of *The Enneagram: A Christian Perspective*

JUANITA CAMPBELL RASMUS
SUZANNE STABILE, SERIES EDITOR

FORTY DAYS ON
BEING A ONE

 ENNEAGRAM DAILY REFLECTIONS

ivp

An imprint of InterVarsity Press
Downers Grove, Illinois

InterVarsity Press
P.O. Box 1400, Downers Grove, IL 60515-1426
ivpress.com
email@ivpress.com

InterVarsity Press® is the book-publishing division of InterVarsity Christian Fellowship/USA®, a movement of students and faculty active on campus at hundreds of universities, colleges, and schools of nursing in the United States of America, and a member movement of the International Fellowship of Evangelical Students. For information about local and regional activities, visit intervarsity.org.

Enneagram figure by InterVarsity Press

Cover design and image composite: David Fassett
Interior design: Daniel van Loon
Images: gold foil background: © Katsumi Murouchi / Moment Collection / Getty Images
*   paper texture background: © Matthieu Tuffet / iStock / Getty Images Plus*

ISBN 978-0-8308-4742-6 (print)
ISBN 978-0-8308-4743-3 (digital)

Printed in the United States of America ∞

Library of Congress Cataloging-in-Publication Data
A catalog record for this book is available from the Library of Congress.

P 20 19 18 17 16 15 14 13 12 11 10 9 8 7 6 5 4 3 2 1
Y 38 37 36 35 34 33 32 31 30 29 28 27 26 25 24 23 22 21

This writing is dedicated
to the C. G. Jung Center in Houston,
and especially to Sister Mary Dennison and
the Spiritual Direction Institute at
Cenacle Retreat Center who provided insight
into the gifts of the Enneagram.

WELCOME TO
ENNEAGRAM DAILY REFLECTIONS

Suzanne Stabile

The Enneagram is about nine ways of seeing. The reflections in this series are written from each of those nine ways of seeing. You have a rare opportunity, while reading and thinking about the experiences shared by each author, to expand your understanding of how they see themselves and how they experience others.

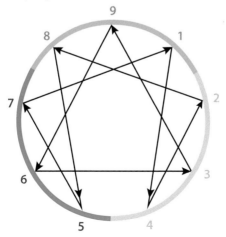

I've committed to teaching the Enneagram, in part, because I believe every person wants at least these two things: to belong, and to live a life that has meaning. And I'm sure that learning and working with the Enneagram has the potential to help all of us with both.

Belonging is complicated. We all want it, but few of us really understand it. The Enneagram identifies—with more accuracy than any other wisdom tool I know—why we can achieve belonging more easily with some people than with others. And it teaches us to find our place in situations and groups without having to displace someone else. (I'm actually convinced that it's the answer to world peace, but some have suggested that I could be exaggerating just a bit.)

If our lives are to have meaning beyond ourselves, we will have to develop the capacity to understand, value, and respect people who see the world differently than we do. We will have to learn to name our own gifts and identify our weaknesses, and the Enneagram reveals both at the same time.

The idea that we are all pretty much alike is shattered by the end of an introductory Enneagram workshop or after reading the last page of a good primer. But for those who are teachable and open to receiving Enneagram wisdom about each of the nine personality types, the shock is accompanied by a beautiful and unexpected gift: they find that they have more compassion for themselves and more grace for others and it's a guarantee.

The authors in this series, representing the nine Enneagram types, have used that compassion to move toward a greater understanding of themselves and others whose lives intersect with theirs in big and small ways. They write from experiences that reflect racial and cultural differences, and they have been influenced by their personal faith commitments. In working with spiritual directors, therapists, and pastors they identified many of their own habits and fears, behaviors and motivations, gifts and challenges. And they courageously talked with those who are close to them about how they are seen and experienced in relationship.

As you begin reading, I think it will be helpful for you to be generous with yourself. Reflect on your own life—where you've been and where you're going. And I hope you will consider the difference between change and transformation. *Change* is when we take on something new. *Transformation* occurs when something old falls away, usually beyond our control. When we see a movie, read a book, or perhaps hear a sermon that we believe "changed our lives," it will seldom, if ever, become transformative. It's a good thing and we may have learned a valuable life lesson, but that's not transformation. Transformation occurs when you have an experience that changes the way you understand life and its mysteries.

When my dad died, I immediately looked for the leather journal I had given to him years before with the request that he fill it with stories and things he wanted me to know. He had only written on one page:

Anything I have achieved or accomplished
in my life is because of the gift of your mother
as my wife. You should get to know her.

I thought I knew her, but I followed his advice, and it was one of the most transformative experiences of my life.

From a place of vulnerability and generosity, each author in this series invites us to walk with them for forty days on their journeys toward transformation. I hope you will not limit your reading to only your number. Read about your spouse or a friend. Consider reading about the type you suspect represents your parents or your siblings. You might even want to read about someone you have little affection for but are willing to try to understand.

You can never change *how* you see, but you can change what you *do* with how you see.

ON BEING A ONE

I am a number One on the Enneagram. If you are a One, you know the weight of the world we carry. If you know a One, these readings will give you enhanced insight into our world. Either way, bring your work boots—you will need them!

My hope is that this book will shine a light on Ones and offer space for some "Yeahs" and "You mean I'm not the only One?" Give yourself permission to reflect on what might offer you more joy and spontaneity, peace of mind, and, dare I just say it up front, more freedom?

I started my Enneagram journey as part of a quest to know who I really was after experiencing a major depressive episode that shattered my sense of self. I lovingly refer to that episode and time in my life as "the crash." What I learned about depression is that when Ones give up on themselves or others, they move to the low side of Enneagram Four behavior. At this point Ones often appear to be depressed to others. And some Ones (like me) do indeed become clinically depressed.

As I was recovering, I attended an Enneagram workshop in Houston, my hometown, at the Jung Center. I almost burst into tears as the facilitator spoke and unpacked my baggage over a few hours. I left the workshop feeling understood and poised for one of the most significant transformations that I would experience in the aftermath of my crash.

Now, some might say that the Enneagram is simply a personality profile, but I would suggest that the Enneagram is a life-transforming insight into a way of living more deeply, richly, and ultimately in a more gratifying way. The Enneagram has been a door, a gate, and a light. It's no coincidence that these same words are also biblical references to Jesus. I am so grateful that the Spirit of God led me to that workshop at the Jung Center, because the insights I gained have given me hope for living the life Jesus assures us of—what Scripture calls the abundant life.

I wrote this in isolation without the counsel of other beautiful Ones to support or deny my claims, so I would love your take on the One you know or the One you are. Join me on social media and let's get talking!

Each day's reading will conclude with a section that you can use however is the most helpful for you—whether making it a time of journaling, self-affirmation, or forging a new practice. Feel free to explore them and see where they take you; do what nurtures your soul.

NOTICE WHAT YOU ARE NOTICING

NOT LONG AGO, MY HUSBAND, Rudy, and I agreed that it was time to make a shift from our busy lives since our way of living wasn't working anymore. I had been living for six months in Indianapolis to support our daughter and son-in-love in caring for our newborn grandson. I had never imagined being a grandmother. I had never dreamed of moving to Indianapolis or living anywhere other than Houston. After six months of Rudy commuting back and forth from Houston, we had a moment of awareness. We noticed that we had too much house in Houston for the shift that had occurred in this new season of our lives, so we downsized.

In Indianapolis, we purchased a small one-bedroom condominium in the complex where our kids lived so that my support for them didn't trespass against them or me. I am an introvert, and I need my space, silence, and solitude. Our little condo is in the lower level of a converted elementary school.

In Houston, we had previously purchased a much smaller home, a foreclosure in our old neighborhood next door to my eighty-eight-year-old mother-in-love. The plan was for it to be our rental for additional income; instead, it became our perfect new home. Rudy and our dear friend Willie Barnes worked on updating the house while I was away in Indy. They did an incredible job with Rudy's eye for design and Willie's craftsmanship. I am happy here in our new home.

This new home is the physical symbol of the significant change occurring in our lives. I have noticed that the reduced square footage makes this house comfy, cozy, and more intimate. I am enjoying that. It is an older home, so we have a front porch, something many houses no longer offer. We have made it a habit to sit on the porch in our rocking chairs, enjoying a glass of evening wine or hot morning tea—just being together, sometimes in silence and other times in raucous laughter. I notice that we are reconnecting with ourselves and our neighbors. Front porches can do that.

I enjoy gardening, and this house has just enough space along the north side of our driveway for a small, above-ground, organic vegetable garden. I planted kale, tomatoes, romaine lettuce, swiss chard, and jalapeños for my hubby. I notice how he loves picking his peppers fresh from our garden, something that has become a lil' bit of joy for him. I invested in a garden plan for our clean slate of a backyard, and it is allowing us to take our time and plant together the fruit trees and flowers that we both had as children and around which we have fond memories. I wanted to attract butterflies to our garden, and we have been able to watch a dozen or so caterpillars eating their way toward transformation.

I have felt such joy here, and I notice that it has been good for our souls in all the right ways. Transformation or change doesn't have to be fraught with anxiety, friction, and chaos. Sometimes change is announcing itself as a conscious choice to notice what we are noticing.

Ones typically ignore or suppress what might have been sublime moments had we been present to them rather than checking the moment off of our to-do list. I am learning how to be present with my noticing, and it is creating such awareness that I can be open to knowing joy.

Sometimes the call for transformation happens suddenly with an announcement; other times it is a subtle shifting of energies or interest. How is your life inviting you into a new way of being?

LETTING GO OF OUR TRY HARDER

AFTER A WEEKLONG VISIT TO INDY, we returned to our home in Houston and I walked into the house as I typically do, settling into my routine, which includes opening the blinds and airing out the house, letting in some fresh air and sunlight.

I opened the blind nearest to the kitchen table and was shocked and startled to find a full-sized blue jay dead on the windowsill. It had come in through the fireplace and couldn't find its way back up and out. My heart went out to it. I imagined how desperately it must have tried to break through the glass. I wondered how long it had fought to live, stuck as it were. I saw the signs against the window where it had beat its breast, hoping to be free. I imagined how terrified it might have felt, not knowing any other way than to "try harder."

We Ones are so like the blue jay trapped in a pattern of "trying harder," and like the blue jay, we die a little every day until we come to see that our way simply doesn't work.

For much of my life, I was trapped in a life of doing-more, pushing-more energy—a just-try-harder kind of mental model. That way of being left me exhausted, depleted, and obsessed. In his book *You2*, Price Pritchett wrote, "If you stake your hopes for a breakthrough on trying harder than ever, you may kill your chances for success."

What if the blue jay had stopped, looked, and listened? Would that the bird had stopped long enough to let go of its tunnel-vision, try-harder mentality. What if it had looked around at how it had flown in? Would that it had listened to the internal compass that is built in its DNA that allows it to migrate seasonally with such great success. No doubt, the blue jay could have found its way to freedom and real life.

What do you and the blue jay have in common?

How are your current challenges or opportunities inviting you into something different?

What would it look like for you to stop, look, and listen to your internal GPS, the Divine speaking in and to you now?

LEARNING TO BE
A LISTENER

I ENGAGE IN SEVERAL WAYS of being present that reflect my spirituality. I am a teacher, preacher, and lifelong learner. I am a pray-er and a listener, and I bring those ways of being to my relationships with God and others. Despite much practice, these ways of being have not always been so well developed, especially the listening part. The One in me has yearned to be heard, validated, seen as right, capable of offering something "valuable" to the conversation, and accepted and approved by those within earshot.

After a significant number of misunderstandings, my error has been that I have not been trained to listen. You see, I had prepared myself to talk, step into the conversation, and be ready with the next word. That had become my pattern, even though I do recall my father's warning "to do twice as much listening as talking." He rationalized that God had equipped me with two ears and one mouth. I am learning that my Oneness wants to be in the conversation at all costs.

Silence, solitude, and an ever-increasing desire to grow in God's grace has spurred me to find a better way to be present with others in my home and the world. I am learning the joy of walking away knowing more about the other than they know about me. I am learning what it means to notice my breathing while others are speaking and to intentionally practice being present to the other.

Unwittingly, my daughters have helped me with this new skill. I have slowly realized that they no longer need my answers as much as they simply need just my active presence. Now they call and say, "Can I vent?" That's my cue to sit down and—in my own words, not theirs—shut up!

It's been amazing, and I have learned so much by taking this approach. In many ways, it lets me off the hook; I don't have to know it all, fix it all, or rescue anyone. Buddhist monk Thich Nhat Hanh says that deep, compassionate listening helps the other to empty their heart, and it gives the other the chance to suffer less. As I am learning to practice listening, I find that I am far more present to others, myself, and God.

Is there a word, phrase, or image here that speaks directly to your experience?

What helps you to be free to be present in the moment?

WHO DIED AND MADE
ONES THE JUDGE?

MATTHEW 7:1 SAYS, "Do not judge, or you too will be judged." Matthew 7:1-5 is Jesus' treatise on condemnation, estimating and sizing up folks, and it is really quite clear. Jesus says that we Ones are setting ourselves up for the big fall, our own consequences grown out of casting judgment on others. The truth is that judging others has been at the basis of probably every major relationship interruption in my life. I had never realized that for me to be "Ms. Right" automatically made the other wrong.

What I'm learning is that condemnation, criticism, and judgment have an energy frequency composed of feelings as far-reaching as fear, hatred, and scorn, which are not life-giving. When I live in judgment instead of paying attention to the truth, something in me dies. Judgment is like sentencing something or, too often, someone to a death they do not deserve. More honestly, what dies is my capacity for compassion for myself and ultimately compassion for others. There is the lesson that, even in my suffering, it's not necessary to destroy, demote, or humiliate those who do not live life according to my stern set of rules, expectations, or notions.

When I'm doing my own inner work of seeking truth, I hear Jesus say, "Who among you is without sin?" I stand watching as Jesus writes on the tablet of my heart and frees me to leave the mob scene of John 8 and go and sin no more. I'm learning that I am the woman caught in adultery, brought to Jesus so he could pronounce judgment on me— and even worse, I'm also the men who want to stone her! Critics from without or within can be murderous, and if I don't listen as Jesus speaks, I can't gain my freedom, as the ones did who were present with Jesus that day.

Read aloud Matthew 7:1-5 and make it personal: "I do not judge, or I too will be judged . . . " What do you notice? How do you feel after reading the text out loud?

Now rewrite the passage in the affirmative: "What can I say to my neighbor instead of, 'Let me take the speck out' . . . ?" What do you notice? How do you feel after rewriting the text? Did any particular memory come to mind, any particular neighbor?

Return to this text and reflect on it again before bed, and just notice what you notice. Take notes.

YOU'D BETTER BE BUSY!

THE ENNEAGRAM SHOWS how each of us is rooted in God. Our challenge is to show the image of God without our dark side taking over.

As an authentic One, I'm a perfectionist and performance addict. These really are about trying to emulate the perfect image of God, yet a bunch of crap gets in the way—stuff such as judgment, self-righteousness, intolerance, and inflexibility.

Recently, my cousin Ricky told me, "You were so bossy when we were kids." Yeah, he was absolutely right about that.

I apologized, "I was just a kid, please forgive me."

While I'm at it, I might as well apologize to all the people I have ever offended. Ones at our worst are bossy as hell and think we are the only ones capable of getting this whole thing worked out to the glory of God! The rest of y'all are just messing around. Don't you know that Jesus is coming back? You better not just *look* busy, but you better *be* busy about the kingdom, or you're going to rot in hell for a very long time. You know that, right?

Yeah, I'm a One. God help me. Please and thank you.

Ones aren't trying to take over everything; we simply have an eye for what appears to be right, in order, and well-perfected—and we tend to be fairly verbal about it. My family often jokes at how, when watching a movie on movie night, I have an eye for seeing the misplaced boom mics and bad edits in a film, noticing the set changes that no one else sees . . . it's the burden of being a One.

What has busyness cost you in energy and capacity to be in relationship?

In what ways has your "doing" taken away from your ability to simply "be" present, open, aware of the impact of how others experience you?

THE "I" IN PRIDE

THE BOOK OF JAMES SPEAKS ABOUT our need to avoid divisive distinctions and partiality: "Believers in humble circumstances ought to take pride in their high position. But the rich should take pride in their humiliation—since they will pass away like a wild flower. For the sun rises with scorching heat and withers the plant; its blossom falls and its beauty is destroyed. In the same way, the rich will fade away even while they go about their business" (James 1:9-11). It's clear that James believes that our relationship as apprentice to Jesus Christ levels all the lines of class and socioeconomics—and I will add ethnicity, race, creed, color, gender, and sexual orientation to that list. James is saying *no* to society's pride of place or the pride felt by Ones due to their positions in the world. Any One reading this undoubtedly agrees with the text on the surface level, right? I mean, because it's the right thing to do, after all. But what does it look like when I'm in the marketplace, and I can allow or forbid others access to the accoutrements that "I have worked hard for, that I have earned" (see Romans 4:4)?

Early on in my career, the Spirit would often call me into the principal's office, so to speak, and invite me to check my pride at the door. I would be given the opportunity to see that my "I" was showing. For so long, the way I kept score in life was to go through my "I don't" list of rules and then compare and exclude others based on my "I." Maybe that's why James begins with, "Consider it pure joy, my brothers and sisters, whenever you face trials of many kinds, because you know that the testing of your faith produces perseverance. Let perseverance finish its work so that you may be mature and complete, not lacking anything" (James 1:1-4).

When I'm living out of the "I" of my life, I find that my relationships get tested, and I seem to suffer more with both the up-close relationships and the more distant ones. The "I" in *pride* is placed exactly in the middle of the word, kind of like "all *Is* on *me*." When I am living out of my "all *Is* on me" space, I inadvertently create divisive distinctions. I move so effortlessly into being the authority of all things, ruling over others, setting up my queendom, and acting as if my contribution or effort is the only solution or way of being in the world. I push out the kingdom of God. I make assumptions about the value of my contributions and the diminished values that others offer. And everybody knows what they say about the word *assume*: it makes an "*ass* out of *u* and *me*."

Distinctions and partiality are rooted in scarcity and in-adequacy. Pride is grounded by each of these notions of "not enough." Think about it: scarcity is "I don't have enough," and inadequacy is "I'm not enough." Each of these is a kind of personal suffering often present while I am unaware of their effect on me and, in turn, how I am affecting others. The times when I have noticed what was going on with me internally have been the times that I have found one or the other, or sometimes both of them, operating in my subconscious. The egoistic pride creates discord in my relationships, and I'm learning to be present to what the trials are seeking to teach me—how they stretch and move me into a more authentic sense of my value and worth, and how I can value and be present to others in a more affirming, life-giving way. I am not diminished by the gifts of the other; I am not less than because the other has more than me. I am experiencing new levels of maturity and awareness. I am growing up, I am finding that I am more present to what is real, and I am learning that the universe is a far more abundant and generous place than I had imagined.

Read James 1:9-11 and 2:1-9. What stands out for you?

I GIVE MYSELF PERMISSION TO BE IN THE MOMENT

I WOKE UP THIS MORNING and remembered to smile first thing! As a rule, I smile to set the tone for my day. I smiled and heard the birds chirping outside my bedroom window. I'd left it ajar just for the possibility of this morning song.

Minutes after I opened my eyes, my hubby, who had awakened earlier, walked in and said, "I think you should stay in bed for as long as you like. I'll bring you whatever you want or need." I took a deep breath and sunk more deeply into our bed. I gave myself permission to just be.

I am typically rigorous about rising early, dressing, having my meditation time, and getting on with the business of the day. But not this morning. I had gone to bed exhausted, having heard too much, seen too much, and felt too much. I declared to my mind that I would awaken happy, healthy, and terrific. And so I did. But I also awoke with the need to nurture myself. I guess Rudy sensed it and thus his offer to care for me that morning.

Ones can drive ourselves to the edge of crazy with our tendencies to sacrifice self-care, fun, spontaneity, and anything that means joy and happiness. Ones typically prioritize work before pleasure, and thus miss out on the beauty of a myriad of opportunities for re-creation and recreation.

I allowed myself to chill and be still. I paid attention to the effects of rain outside my window, noticing the sky and its pillows of gray, and I thought, "I'm not moving out of bed, not yet anyway. I'm declaring pajama day or perhaps half-day! I'm breaking all my rules around morning ritual and morning routines. I'm having my tea in bed along with a piece of fruit. I've got a book, my phone, and as best I can tell, all is still well with the world. Today I'm choosing being in bed as a way of self-care. I'll stay in a lil' longer, and at some point I'll decide that I'm ready to open for business."

We Ones can learn the freedom of calling our own timeouts—time for fun, time for wonder, time for rest, for recreation, for hobbies, or for something of interest like the book on my bed. We are the only authority over our thinking, actions, feeling choices, and quality of living. The chief way we Ones learn to live more expansively is by granting ourselves permission to practice being in the moment, plain and simple!

The Dalai Lama once said, "If you want others to be happy, practice compassion. If you want to be happy, practice compassion." How do you need to give yourself permission to love, accept, and approve of yourself, and to practice self-care, self-nurturing, and self-compassion?

GOD RESTORES
MY SOUL

THE GIFT OF THE ENNEAGRAM has been the ability to sit with the aspects of my shadow self that I have avoided over the years and to know them by name. It has been humbling to see how my way of being an unhealthy One has affected my relationships and perpetuated my experiences of pain in relationships. I have been able to name my culpability, where in the not too distant past I had only seen the faults of others. As we Ones seek to mature in our life with God, we are given the ability to see. I now see more clearly how my need to be right has at times been crushingly offensive to others I had damned in my mind. I also see why David could write in Psalm 23 that we have in God a shepherd who can restore our souls.

I am flooded with humility when I am able to see how many times my righteousness has left others hurt and distanced from me, and possibly distanced me from my relationship with God as I lead as a pastor. It humbles me when I recall instances where I was not my best self and how the shadow side in my unhealthy state left others wounded. The good news has been that I can ask the other to forgive me where it is physically and emotionally safe to do so. And I can slow down and take the time to repent before God and then allow God to heal in me what needs healing, what needs a new perspective, and what needs total restoration in my soul—and, I pray, in the soul of the other as well.

When I am willing, God is able. I am experiencing that grace as God has shown me wounds that I created in my daughters out of my need to be perceived as a perfect mother. It's been mind-blowing to recognize that my motives were all about me looking good, and that their behavior and appearances in their formidable years were all about how they reflected on me. I was clueless to my own underlying needs and motivations. Family systems theory teaches that parents through generations unconsciously transmit their own soul wounds in a gamut of unhealthy ways to their children, and it isn't until they become self-aware and learn to manage their own reactivity that they begin to have less pain-driven, more differentiated, and healthier relationships. Like other vocations, parenting is one more arena of learning to be and do better.

In my journey, it has been therapy, God's tactful promptings, and awakenings along the way that have helped me ask for forgiveness, especially when I see how my past thinking affected my daughters. They have been so gracious to me. As they in turn have grown in their own healing processes, they have offered me so much forgiveness and tenderness. Parallel with Scripture, the Enneagram invites us to seek healing, and I am forever grateful for mine. An added gift has been that the process has paid off in my relationships with my now adult daughters. So, I can say that God not only is restoring my soul, but God is also allowing my daughters' souls to be restored as well.

Ones don't want to be wrong, and that can be the weightiest baggage ever. What we often need is to be conscious of God's grace available to us. That means slowing down to notice what we are feeling, to notice what seems to be driving our decisions and interactions. Others often can name our soul wounds much better than we can. But we too can grow to notice them and work with God to experience various levels of restoration. Therapy and taking time to notice has been an amazing source of God's grace for me. What will work for you to allow God to restore your soul?

THE GOD OF
RELATIONSHIPS

MONTHS BEFORE MY CRASH, I heard the word "rest" in my soul. It wasn't as though there was an alarm of any sort, just a still, small voice. Several times in the course of weeks prior to my crash, I heard "rest" as the invitation I was being offered. I could look back over that time and regret that I didn't pay attention, but that would be a futile exercise and a waste of life energy. What I learned through reflecting on that time was that I never investigated what God meant by "rest."

You see, I have at times made a great number of assumptions about "words" I've heard from God. The primary and most devastating one has been the assumption that I knew exactly what God was saying. I had translated rest to mean I needed a nap, that perhaps I was sleepy. So, I totally ignored any warning because I didn't feel sleepy—quite the contrary, I was wired up way too tight.

I never once said, "God, what are you saying to me?" I believe that if I had inquired, God would have given me some measure of insight. Mine was surely a case of making assumptions.

Here's what I'm finally learning: God is interested in relationships, including the one with me. That means dialogue and interaction with God, as we do with friends. I often would hear a word and then go running off to obey the word without any clarity about what the word meant, whether timing was relative, or even if the word was for me. So many mistakes! Much of that way of acting was rooted in my validating myself by my "doing-ness" instead of my "being-ness."

I'm learning that when God speaks, it's wise to take the Mary approach (of Mary and Martha fame) and sit with Jesus and ask for clarity. It's time to stop being busy to get attention and start being quiet so Jesus can cherish me just because. Similar to our best human relationships, sometimes it's time to just listen to the other to understand rather than to respond.

Scripture tells us, "Let the beloved of the LORD rest secure in him, for he shields him all day long" (Deuteronomy 33:12).

What I'm learning is a new way to be with God: the way of inquiry, the way of being still, the way of simple listening and asking. It's an old school style dialogue where I'm getting to know the heart of God, not just chasing directives I believe I've been given. I am finding that God desires friendship, collaboration, stillness, and even silence while we sit together co-creating notions of what's next and what's best. The word "rest" that God spoke was an invitation for me to know a new way of being. It was to know freedom from my hardworking Oneness and enter into a life-transforming way of being that would give me rest and freedom from the addiction to and identity of incessant doing. It was freedom from my overwhelming expectations of myself and others—freedom to know that I was loved by God and that was enough. God has been offering me a childlike freedom to spontaneity, optimism, enthusiasm, and creativity. My old way had closed off my access to all the really good God stuff. I am so grateful that God is patiently teaching me what it means to rest.

Read John 13:1-10. How can you be more open to being the recipient of God's love and care, to allow your feet to be washed, like Jesus washed the feet of his disciples? David Benner wrote in *Conversations* (Fall/Winter 2010), "Consent is the first and most important step to receiving God's grace."

WE JUST WANT TO BUILD
A BETTER WORLD

IF ONES WERE CARPENTERS building the world, our preferred tool probably would be a hammer. We would want to hammer out the imperfections of the world. We would then hammer in rightness, morality, competence, integrity, fairness, and justice. We would hammer in the qualities that we so value and for which we believe we hold ourselves accountable. But as you can imagine, not everything can or should be hammered.

There are the more delicate things that need a mallet with its wider head and ability to leave its object unmarred. Of course, there is an array of other tools that make building and repairing things possible. Not everyone responds to being hammered on our points of rightness, goodness, and perfectness. Some things are best managed with a screwdriver, or a saw, or even glue, which might be the preferred carpenter's tool.

As a One, I'm learning to notice when I come on too strong with my way as *the* way, as though no other ways are even possible or plausible. Yes, unfortunately, I've hammered more than a few folks with my absolutes, rules, and mandates. My children have probably suffered most from this way of seeing life. My conviction to what I believe is the right way to do or to be can be downright demolishing to the other. For Ones, rules can be more important to us at times than being in relationship.

Ones are not usually gentle with themselves, and that can be descriptive of why they can be so hard on others. We haven't learned to love ourselves well, so we don't always know how to love our neighbors well. But the good news is that many Ones are natural teachers and once we get an idea, concept, or new insight, we go to town with implementing it as faithful, lifelong learners.

While our nature is still at work to save the world, we are here to show the goodness of God. Our task as Ones is to come to know that only when we ourselves are at union with God, and abiding in God, are we freer to be a truly good person. Our growth comes in seeing that it's not something we have to force, instead it's a way we can learn to be. Our potential for goodness is in our DNA.

We Ones have an eye for what needs fixing, improving, and changing. The harmony comes in seeing that there exists among us some really beautiful people who are also being guided by the same God who is guiding us. Indeed, we are here to inspire others to be their best selves, to exercise their creativity, and to encourage them to offer the world their own unique way of being. At our best, Ones are conscientious, can be counted on, and are often committed to a life of service.

When we are operating in harmony with the Divine, we become better able to see and build a better world in all the best ways. Richard Rohr wrote in *Just This*, "The contemplative mind does not tell us *what* to see; it teaches us *how* to see what we behold."

What tools are being used by God to bring insight and awareness in you?

What tools would be helpful to you as you seek to serve and guide others?

SOME RULES ARE MEANT TO BE BROKEN

DURING THE COVID-19 CRISIS, new social rules of engagement were constructed to care for oneself and neighbor. It required a major adjustment to new norms. So, to care for our neighbors during the pandemic meant breaking with traditional ways that we relate in community, like hugging and shaking hands.

All of this reminded me of the familiar parable told by Jesus about the Good Samaritan (Luke 10:30-37). A man had been robbed, beaten, and left to die by the side of the road. A priest and a Levite—the good Christians of the day—passed by without helping. But a Samaritan stopped, took him to a shelter to get him help, and even paid the bill. Most think the lesson is simply about being a good neighbor, as Jesus points out, but I wonder if the bigger lesson is being a good neighbor despite what the cultural rules say.

In this case, the message to the Samaritan was "you aren't welcome in that neighborhood." Jews despised Samaritans, so Jews would travel out of their way to avoid contact.

Now in all honesty, we Christians have been really hard on the two church folks who passed to the other side of the road to avoid breaking their cultural religious rules about touching the unclean and avoiding dead bodies. It is so easy to judge those guys at a distance of two thousand–plus years, isn't it? But at the same time, we Ones get it, because the rules are the rules, right? Or are they?

To the people listening to Jesus' story, the Samaritan definitely was not their culturally accepted choice for a hero, yet he acted heroically by walking straight toward the brutalized man and showing him compassion. He broke all the cultural rules between Jews and Samaritans. I wonder if Jesus was saying that relationship supersedes the rules—in essence, that some rules are meant to be broken? Clearly, Jesus celebrates the Samaritan and then says to the audience, "Which one was a neighbor? Now go and be neighbors." I believe that Jesus also was giving the audience permission to break the rules and, in so doing, to enter into the possibility of transformation. Jesus was using an object lesson to awaken the legalistic rule followers to a more superior reality—the reality of the availability of the kingdom of God, the innermost spiritual authority of love, compassion, kindness, and goodness because "against such things there is no law" (Galatians 5:23).

Can you think of a time when you were on your way to work, an appointment, or worship services when you were suddenly moved by someone in need? How did you respond? Did you stick to the familiar or did you break your rule to render aid? How did your choice leave you feeling? Write about your reflections.

ALL BOXED IN

COULD IT BE THAT GOD is using the Enneagram as a crow bar, a means of opening self-reflection and growth?

During one particularly difficult time in my life, I remember God saying, "Juanita, you have boxed yourself in and boxed me out." I had no idea what that meant at the time, but as I pondered what God was saying, I came to see that I had become my own little demigod. I had imagined that my rules were *the* rules, primarily because I had enhanced my rules to assure that I didn't break God's big ten—the commandments, that is. This all started in childhood as my ideal "good little girl" was being cultivated and trained up.

Over time, the Enneagram has helped me to see that I had indeed boxed myself in with all my "thou shalt not" rules—but rarely were there any "by all means thou shall" rules I followed. My box was built out of many things: the need to avoid punishment, feeling disappointed in myself or others because we Ones have high expectations, feeling underappreciated, and often feeling upset and angry, which comes from feeling that others aren't carrying their weight in a role or relationship. My box was tenuously held together by strings of tension and anxiety that Ones just kind of assume we are expected to live with.

The good news is that we Ones can begin to deconstruct our boxes by acknowledging that we created the boxes out of which we have lived, and with God's help, we can deconstruct all that no longer serves us. To answer my initial question: yes, I believe we are being invited to use our new "Enneagram crow bar" to pry open a much more expansive way of living.

In John 12:23-26, Jesus speaks about the necessity of a kernel of wheat falling to the ground, dying, and then bearing much fruit. I think he's trying to tell us that we can crack open our boxes to become our best selves, our most fruitful selves. Our boxes have been made up of thoughts, and those thoughts can be changed. The same wood that was used to make a box can make a crib or a chair. New possibilities are made available when we are willing to surrender our way of being for God's way, which is fruitfulness.

Can you be more open to and more trusting of God's plan for you—to love and transform yourself; to help you love, accept, and approve of yourself; and to lead you into a more expansive way of being in the world? What comprises the box that holds you, and how can you deconstruct it?

WHERE IS
THE JOY?

ONES VALUE LEARNING, and that includes gaining new perspectives on our lives and our contribution and place in the world. We may not enjoy any of what we believe we ought to or should be doing because we often have siphoned off joy as a trade for responsibility that can be rewarded and measured. Rarely have we focused on the benefits or qualities of the fruit of the Spirit, joy being one of them. The 1972 song "Where Is the Love" sung by Roberta Flack and Donny Hathaway asks, "Where is the love you said you'd give to me soon as you were free? Will it ever be? Where is the love?" For Ones, the song is, "Where is the joy?"

We are often too serious, too focused, and too hard working to even recognize that our lives are wound up too tight and not even a hint of joy lingers in our midst. Our doings become mere obligations to be checked off our to-do list. But what about our to *be* list? What about being joyful;

what about ecstasy, bliss, and pleasure? What about creating spaces to allow the flow of the Holy Spirit's joy juice into our being?

Where is the joy? Joy is the place of growth, learning, and transformation for the One. For a long time, I don't think that I was aware of the lack of joy in my life. I felt that I was robbed of my joy in childhood. Joy didn't get rewarded. Adele and Doug Calhoun, and Clare and Scott Loughrige offer this insight in *Spiritual Rhythms for the Enneagram*: "One children try to be perfect and do the right thing. These defenses protected and also mitigated against joyous connectedness and creativity."

I believe that even ingrained unhealthy habits learned in my childhood, rigidity and such, can be unlearned or transformed in the adult me. In *Spiritual Rhythms for the Enneagram*, Ones are encouraged to "practice play." During an extremely low point once, the Spirit asked me what I enjoyed as a child. After some reflection, I recalled that I enjoyed playing, jumping off my grandmother's porch, climbing trees, and riding my bike. As an adult, with help from the Enneagram, I am learning to practice playing. I am blowing more bubbles, riding my bike, coloring, and painting with my adult version of paint-by-numbers. I am even learning to color outside the lines.

C. S. Lewis said, "Joy is the serious business of heaven." That speaks to a One who is learning to play.

Just as the Spirit invited me to reflect on what I enjoyed in childhood, take some time now to ask yourself what you enjoyed playing as a child. How can you translate that to starting to play now? When was the last time you enjoyed planning a trip or laughing with your funny friend? How can you create some playtime every day? Let yourself off the hook today!

STAY OPEN TO JOY

IN HIS BOOK *The Divine Conspiracy*, my dear friend and mentor Dallas Willard wrote about "God's Joyous Being." He recalls a moment of seeing a view in South Africa that was exhilarating and awe-inspiring. He was on a drive, and as he approached a beach, he came to a place where the land and sea opened in vastness. He was mesmerized by the infinite beauty before him. Indeed, he had seen beaches before, but he remarked that in seeing this particular beach he experienced its textures, radiance, and power, and was seized by wonder and amazement.

He reflected on how God gets to see this all the time and how God no doubt must be the most joyous while constantly seeing this magnificence. He wrote, "It is perhaps strange to say, but suddenly I was extremely happy for God and thought I had some sense of what an infinitely joyous consciousness he is and of what it might have meant for him to look at his creation and find it 'very good.'"

There is something transcendent about beauty in nature that has the capacity to open us up to supremely sublime joy.

Whether it's the thunderous sounds of Niagara Falls, the vast blooming meadows of Zimbabwe, the stunning luminous architecture of a four-foot-wide spider's web, or the beauty of seeing a monarch emerging from her chrysalis in front of your eyes, nature invites us to stay open to joy.

So many Scriptures talk about joy. Here are just a few from the ESV:

A joyful heart is good medicine,
    but a crushed spirit dries up the bones.
      (Proverbs 17:22)

These things I have spoken to you, that my joy may be in you, and that your joy may be full. (John 15:11)

For you shall go out in joy
    and be led forth in peace;
the mountains and the hills before you
    shall break forth into singing,
and all the trees of the field shall clap their hands.
      (Isaiah 55:12)

> Our girls grew up with Fun Fridays in their school. Why not claim a day, or perhaps just a couple of hours, and declare your own version of Fun Friday? You can have your playdate alone or with others, in nature or not—you get to choose. Plan your playdate for next week, and

every week, and in thirty days' time, you'll have a habit of making room for *joy*!

After your playdates, write an honest reflection on how the experience gave you life and joy, or took life from you and wasn't what you'd hoped it would be, and so on. Then write a note of gratitude to God for your experience and your learnings.

LETTING GO OF CONDEMNATION

"FOR GOD SO LOVED THE WORLD that he gave his one and only Son, that whoever believes in him shall not perish but have eternal life" (John 3:16). How long have I known this familiar gospel verse? I imagine that I learned it from my maternal grandmother, since she taught me Scripture verses before I could read. I am often amazed how the church is quick to offer verse 16, yet we mumble, stumble, and trip in more ways than one if we are asked to recite verse 17: "For God did not send his Son into the world to condemn the world, but to save the world through him."

It's funny how the worst thing that could happen to you becomes the best possible thing for you. When my world fell apart, I came face-to-face with ways of thinking about myself as a One, which no longer served me. My inner critic, with her well-honed condemnation and crushingly high expectations, fell shattered at my feet. She meant me no good and had served to distract me from coming into relationship with the two people I needed desperately—the authentic me and the real God.

I had been so fixated on rules around integrity and standards that I had begun to believe I was the sum of my expectations, and all that I condemned and judged was a means of clarifying my identity—which it had been, until that point. Not true! All the condemnation and rules did was separate me from knowing my most authentic self, the me who values a little fun and games, the me who likes to take risks, calculated as they may be. I couldn't value the world around me because I was always seeing what seemed wrong, which seems to be the way of the One. Likewise, I couldn't validate my own sense of being because I had imagined that the rules were who I was. Yet John 3:16-17 clearly say I am loved, not condemned, and God has sent Jesus to help me see that the availability of God's love is present to me here and now.

Condemnation is a habit, and habits, like rules, can be broken. God's love made me so very aware that condemnation appeared to be what I was projecting outside of myself. But that condemnation originated in me, and that's where it needed to end. God's overwhelming presence as love helped me become aware that I was being offered a better way to live. Condemnation was an ingredient in the quality of my inner life, but Christ was offering me a way of being that drew no lines of demarcation, and in fact, whose scope was so formidable that it could make room for me and all the limiting beliefs that I would later be challenged to see transformed by God's immeasurable love.

The opposite of God's love is condemnation, when you perceive the other or self without the lens of love. What would it be like for you to gain freedom from condemning yourself? How do you think others will interact with you in such a state of being? Imagine yourself practicing this for thirty consecutive days—would you have a new, healthy, contagious habit?

LOVED, PERIOD!

FOR MANY YEARS I WAS GETTING GOD WRONG. At the core of my belief system was that love wasn't enough. I had been condemned, and only my diligent and dutiful complying to the law would get me in right standing with God. Needless to say, this wasn't conscious thinking. I had to be awakened to the reality of my thought life.

From my worst experiences, I learned that God loved me, period! No report card of righteousness, no failing grades in rule following—God just loved me and wanted desperately for me to know the magnitude of that love. I felt as though I had lived in a body cast for most of my life, and the cast was being removed. I was left exposed and vulnerable, but I was also set free. Who would I be now without my rules of condemnation, judgment, and such? Who would God be (in my mind) if not the One keeping score of my every wrong?

I found out that I was loved, generously, and with great tenderness. I found out that God really was love—pure, accepting, and present, offering to wash my feet and care for me at my weakest moments as I recovered from the weaknesses of the body cast I had grown so accustomed to. I found God, the one who is Emmanuel, kept vigil over me day and night. The one the Jews find so sacred as to only call Yahweh. I found the eternal mother who cared for me as though I were her only child, holding me close to nurture my every need. I found the everlasting Papa who fathered me tirelessly, binding my wounds and healing the wreckage of my brokenness. I found the God who knows no condemnation and has no capacity for it. I found that I was being loved, period, without condemnation, judgment, or sentencing. I found God, the God of love, who placed relationship over rules, oughts, and shoulds.

Read Matthew 3:13-17, but fill in your name instead of the name of Jesus. Try reading it aloud and reflect on any insights you might gain.

Then [your name] came from Galilee to the Jordan to be baptized by John. But John tried to deter him, saying, "I need to be baptized by you, and do you come to me?"

[your name] replied, "Let it be so now; it is proper for us to do this to fulfill all righteousness." Then John consented.

As soon as [your name] was baptized, he went up out of the water. At that moment heaven was opened, and he saw the Spirit of God descending like a dove and alighting on him. And a voice from heaven said, "This is my Son, whom I love; with him I am well pleased."

Imagine yourself in Jesus' place. What is it like to experience the Father's love so personally? To sense God saying to you, "I love you, my child, and I am pleased with you"?

ASK FOR WHAT
YOU NEED

ONES ARE DIE-HARD FANS OF RULES and believe that everything must be in order, but we often have areas where we throw caution to the wind, at least for a time. While most outward appearances will be neat and sometimes even pristine, there will usually be an area in our life that suffers from a lack of discipline or structure. Such has been the case with my home office. I had just finished writing *Learning to Be*, and my home office was a sea wreck of open books, tabbed, stacked, and spread across almost every surface area in its eight-by-ten borders.

I often allow my office to be the place where my rules for order are relaxed, but this place was out of control. In an effort to support my well-being or really just to compare and judge, I looked to social media to do an unofficial check on the status of other writers' workspaces. I was both appalled and sadly comforted when I found a real mix of offices, some of which had been renovated for the camera shoot and others that made me feel that I was in good company with my reckless abandon.

Every morning for weeks, I walked into my office and felt a measure of claustrophobia, overwhelm, and plain old frustration. Typical of a One, I suppressed my feelings and simply worked harder to focus and get 'er done while surrounded by the stifling restrictions of an office overrun by books and papers. My office looked like a massacre had occurred, yet I pressed on toward the mark while an editorial deadline loomed large. Then one morning while I was preparing for my day, the Spirit spoke and said, "Ask Rudy to help you."

I let the words settle in, since as a One I can at times be reticent to ask for help. I'm so accustomed to being the one offering help or support. People begin to assume that we Ones are superbeings and need little to no aid. I walked into my husband's office and said, "Good morning, I need your help!" I explained my situation and asked him to think about solutions. In my mind, there was a credenza to purchase, a carpenter to hire, and more.

That evening, I retired for the night and awoke about 3:00 a.m. to Rudy just getting in bed. He said simply, "Did you see your office?" Of course, I had not, so I headed straightaway to my office. I was blown away. My hubby had worked tirelessly for hours into the wee morning to arrange, stage, organize, and create for me an environment that felt calm, serene, and so joyful that I was speechless. I felt like I could breathe again. Now the physical space was positively affecting my physical and mental well-being. I thanked him profusely, and I am still thanking him.

I will be forever grateful that I asked for help, something we Ones can be hesitant to do. I am learning that asking for help, rather than being a sign of weakness, is an act of self-compassion.

"If you remain in me and my words remain in you, ask whatever you wish, and it will be done for you" (John 15:7). What would you like to ask God for today?

A BREAKFAST FILLED
WITH INADEQUACY

IT WAS A LOVELY, EARLY SPRING Saturday morning. The air was crisp and I was excited about the fun we would have. I had invited my mother-in-love, who we affectionately call MeMe, to join me for a breakfast where I was offering the invocation for a fancy gala. We were dressed in our best spring attire, and optimism filled the car as we headed to the venue. Our timing was perfect, on schedule, just as I had planned. We chatted in the car en route, and we were minutes away from the hotel when I noticed that the highway exit had been closed and all traffic was being rerouted. I was alert but not panicked. I knew the route and we had some time to spare, or so I imagined. What I had not counted on was the exit for the hotel being closed, traffic being rerouted miles out of the way from the freeway onto the streets with their untold traffic signals, and the resulting congestion due to the closed exit.

Morning joy became dread. I had left my home in plenty of time to be in place at the podium, but by the time we valet parked and got to the banquet hall, it was a few minutes after the start time. As fate would have it, they had been prompt and started right on time. The event convener didn't know me, so she didn't know that punctuality was a pet peeve of mine; she didn't know that I prided myself in being on time. She also didn't have any idea of how many folks I'd judged for being late. I felt her pithy disdain when I arrived tardy; it was all in her look.

Is this how I had treated others? Had I rejected those who had been late to my meetings or gatherings in this same way? I felt as though I was four years old and being scolded by stern looks and no words. I felt it the entire breakfast. The room was exquisitely decorated and filled with incredibly coiffured and smiling women, some familiar, yet so many unknown to me. I withered inside, bombarded by feelings of vulnerability, inadequacy, guilt, shame, and alienation.

There was the feeling of embarrassment—not only had I angered the convener, but I had been exposed to a banquet room of people who didn't know me, my reputation for punctuality, or my insistence that tardiness was a habit of personal irresponsibility. Ones are often brutally critical of themselves because we take ourselves so seriously. I imagined the awkward pause if they called my name and I didn't make it to the podium—a gasp, a hushed crowd waiting, the scrambling for someone else to step in. It was too much to sit with. How could I eat after playing that scene over and over in my head? It was all I could do to stay in my seat tall and straight.

No one said anything negative to me about my being tardy. Everything I felt was based on my own core beliefs about who I was. My inner dialogue was all of my own creation.

When have you been overwhelmed by your own inner dialogue? What story were you telling yourself in that moment? My own beliefs about myself had trapped me into feelings of vulnerability, inadequacy, shame, alienation, embarrassment, and guilt. What feelings did you know in your inner dialogue? Our thoughts create our feelings, but we have the power to change our thoughts and change the narrative that surrounds our core beliefs, thus changing our feelings. My narrative has been about securing love and acceptance in exchange for my accomplishments, which can change dramatically when things go right. What about you? What would you like to change about your narrative?

MEME AND REAL LIFE

ON THE WAY HOME FROM the breakfast gala, I was reeling inside. My inner critic was having a field day and no doubt it showed on my countenance. My mother-in-love had sat with me through it all in quiet support, present without comment. Perhaps she had been searching for the right words to say. After a bit more of the kind of silence that allowed me to further bask in shame, MeMe spoke up: "Juanita, this shit ain't real."

Her words cut straight down to my inner critic, who tucked her tail and climbed back into her ego-centered hole. MeMe's words shifted the atmosphere for me. You see, my mother-in-love was experiencing her own measure of what was real.

The real for MeMe was that her husband of forty-five years was dying in hospice. She had agreed to attend the event with me because she needed a different space to break the vigil of pending death. I had hoped the fancy breakfast would bring her a beautiful distraction from her realities. I had hoped to bring her a gift of being surrounded by all things gorgeous and grand for a few hours of respite for her weary soul. But with her little comment, she reminded me that I am human and therefore open to the reality that life is an imperfect place, and sometimes even my best intentions will go awry.

Her words were her way of reminding me that stuff happens beyond our proper planning. There are some things that are simply out of our control, as painful as that is for a One to come to terms with. Her words in that moment brought me out of my pit of self-pity and rejection. Ones do not want to be seen as incompetent or defective. I will always remember her words, not only because I had never before heard her use profanity, but also because her truth shattered my self-loathing and shook me into the awareness that this was not a matter of life and death—not real life anyway.

The following portion of the poem "To a Mouse," written in 1785 by Robert Burns and translated here into standard English, is a classic reminder about plans going wrong:

But little Mouse, you are not alone,
In proving foresight may be vain:
The best laid schemes of mice and men
Go often awry,
And leave us nothing but grief and pain,
For promised joy!

Can you recall a time when things didn't go as planned, and articulate your feelings during the incident?

Just as we can remember well when things went wrong, we also can recall when things went right—when we felt loved, accepted, or approved of—whether that came from a grandparent, teacher, childhood friend, grand-child, or even a pet. Along with reflecting on a difficult time, can you change gears to recall a time when you experienced value, security, forgiveness, or being loved?

THE FULL
SERENITY PRAYER

WHILE MANY HAVE SEEN OR HEARD on various occasions the shorter version of the Serenity Prayer below, made famous thanks to the various global twelve-step programs and originally written by Dr. Reinhold Niebuhr, most have not read the fuller text of the prayer. No doubt, the Serenity Prayer was written with Ones in mind. In fact, it has such important content for Ones that I have focused the next five daily readings on it.

Short version:

God grant me the serenity
To accept the things, I cannot change;
Courage to change the things I can;
And wisdom to know the difference.

Long version:

God grant me the serenity
To accept the things, I cannot change;

Courage to change the things I can;
And wisdom to know the difference.

Living one day at a time;
Enjoying one moment at a time;
Accepting hardships as the pathway to peace;
Taking, as [God] did, this sinful world
As it is, not as I would have it;
Trusting that [God] will make things right
If I surrender to [God's] Will;
So that I may be reasonably happy in this life
And supremely happy with [God]
Forever and ever in the next.
Amen.

"Living one day at a time," the practice of being in the present moment, is so profoundly freeing. When we Ones train ourselves in this mindful awareness, we can enjoy the provision of God that Jesus taught the disciples while teaching them to pray, "give us this day." For us, Jesus consciousness is the awareness that in this moment we have all that is needed for this moment. We become overwhelmed as Ones when we move outside of the here and now. We begin to scare and frighten ourselves when we believe that we will not have enough for the day or be enough in the day. One day at a time is far more than just a good slogan: it is the apex of a belief system that frees the believer from the undue fears of inadequacy and scarcity.

"Enjoying one moment at a time"—now there's a novel notion for us Ones. What if we could open up a bit and learn to cultivate and perhaps even curate a moment of joy? We are prone to pushing off the fun until all the work is done. Often, we Ones are the folks giving the side eye to our colleagues who are goofing off in the midst of times of crisis. "Don't they realize," we mumble, "that this thing is going to be over, and our work deadlines will still need to be met?" We typically come out of crisis situations with no great stories and no heartfelt memories—only a to-do list that may or may not have been completed based on the additional work we felt that needed to be done or should have been accomplished.

Ones can struggle and even wrestle with joy. We need it desperately, but when we are stressed we rarely justify it, believing the cost of joy is too excessive based on our need to be dutiful and seen as responsible. Could this missing piece called joy be the reason we are sometimes seen as rigid and find ourselves resentful? I am recommending a joy break for us Ones. We can start small, maybe with a lil' bottle of bubbles on our desk, and we can set an alarm to remind us to just stop, drop, relax, and blow a few bubbles. We can give our inner child permission for joy. I am learning there are enormous dividends for doing so.

The book of Nehemiah offers this instruction: "Go home and prepare a feast, holiday food and drink; and share it with those who don't have anything: This day is holy to God. Don't feel bad. The joy of GOD is your strength!" (Nehemiah 8:10, *The Message*). Imagine yourself looking in the mirror, smiling, and saying out loud that you are open to the joy of the Lord in your life, that you will allow yourself to relax and take time to enjoy life, that you recognize that God wants you to have joy—and in fact, God says that joy in you is a fruit of the Spirit and also your strength!

ACCEPTANCE

THE LINE IN THE SERENITY PRAYER, "Accepting hardships as the pathway to peace," describes what it's like to live in the moment. What an enlightened way of perceiving and framing hardships. I have never once considered that my hardships were the sidewalks moving me toward peace. Hardships were always the thing I simply wanted to sleep away, or in the case of the feelings that come up during those times, I just wanted to suppress them, stifle their expression and their insight, and move on with the hustle and grind.

We Ones can work our way out of anything; it's what the doer in us does. Acceptance means Ones don't have to fear the hardships nor the feelings that they stir up in us. We can train ourselves to simply be present to our suffering and know that God is indeed working all things together for our good. The Scripture reminds us in Ecclesiastes 3 that there is a time and a season for everything under heaven. Acceptance invites us to reframe our thinking and invites us to wonder: *This must be the time for this hardship. I wonder what treasure it will reveal in me? I wonder how it will perfect my character or transform my thinking in a more expansive way?*

Acceptance is an expansive notion for us Ones. Acceptance means keeping our hearts and minds open to greater and more creative ways of being, like exercising new muscles. Ones are notorious for wanting life to be black or white, right or wrong, or good or bad, even in our hardships. This kind of dualistic thinking sucks the life out of Ones, and joy is often the first casualty. In contrast, the Serenity Prayer admonition is to live one day at a time, to enjoy one moment at a time, and to accept hardships as the pathway to peace. These are all ways of living in the reality of a less than black-and-white world. This more expansive way of thinking means that Ones are invited to live in varying shades of gray. We can be seen by others as closed-minded, but learning acceptance is a practice that can open our minds to living beyond our limited life inside of the lines we've drawn and the rules we've claimed.

The notion of accepting hardships as the pathway to peace is an invitation for Ones to stay open to being surprised by the possibilities of good flowing from the most unlikely places. We then must let go of our notions of all good or all bad and be willing to see that hardships and suffering have the capacity to offer us the gift of inner peace. We are invited to let go of judging our experiences and labeling them; we are invited to see the treasure in the darkness. Acceptance means letting go of having life our way.

For too long, I had assumed that my rule following and line drawing—my black-or-white, good-or-bad, right-or-wrong thinking—would help me avoid suffering and hardship. It has not. Being a Christian doesn't give me a pass from hardship or suffering. Until I hit bottom, my old thinking paradigm ruled my world.

Take some time and soak in this part of the Serenity Prayer, or grab some paper and write it out, perhaps in a letter that you mail to yourself, or say it out loud until you memorize the words. There is a lot here to unpack, so give yourself some time to find the most creative way that works for you to think, ruminate, pray, reflect, and articulate.

Accepting hardships as the pathway to peace;
Taking, as [God] did, this sinful world
As it is, not as I would have it;
Trusting that [God] will make things right
If I surrender to [God's] Will.

THE GOD WHO MAKES THINGS RIGHT

THE CORE BELIEF OF ONES is that the world around us is flawed; we live with that belief starting with childhood. Over a lifetime, we gather such sufficient data that our recorded memory believes this to be the absolute gospel, that the world needs the critical insight that we Ones bring. We live in the world knowing, based on our beliefs and the evidence we've collected through our experiences, that there is always room for improvement.

We rarely see things as being good enough. We all know this way of thinking is subconscious, so stay open to the insight available to us as we reflect on this together.

Ones have become so accustomed to depending on our gifts of efficiency, reliability, work ethic, talents, and capacity that unknowingly we are often far more reliant on our own abilities than on the power of God operating in and through us. We tend to trust that we will make things right, rather than trusting that God will make things right, because we think God has far more critical things to resolve.

That self-dependency rarely disappoints until it does, and then, as we hit a new low, we Ones find ourselves starting life all over again. Ones are prone to trust what we know, and often it is not a trust in knowing God. So, trusting that God will make it right is an invitation for us to surrender our own will for the will of God. It means letting go of our understanding of how we think things ought to be, should be, and would be—the right way to be. All that goes out the window when prayer is a conscious decision to align our minds to the mind and will of Christ.

To trust that God will make things right means we are willing to pay attention to who we have believed God to be. The God of my understanding prior to my all-time low crash point was a judgmental and punitive God—a tough taskmaster, a cross between Judge Judy and Santa Claus, checking the list to see if I was naughty or nice. In the darkness of my worst trial, my image of "god" was darkened also.

Thank God for those trials, though, because I was able to come to know the God of love and compassion, one who faithfully loved me, even in my impotence and vulnerability. This God sat with me and washed my feet with loving tenderness, all the while comforting me with words of hope and sometimes even humor. This God helped me to see without any condescension or criticism that every need I had and every longing would be attended to. Day after day in the solitude and silence of recovery, I was afforded new ways of being with God, and I gained a solid awareness that

God could be trusted. My image and understanding of who God is and how God is trustworthy has been amazingly transformed. My lowest time gave me the opportunity to grow up and to grow my image of God, the one who redeems us at our worst and makes things right.

How does this reading intersect with your life today? What phrase or word stands out for you in this reading? Is there an invitation? How will you respond?

A few things to imagine as you reflect: trust God in every area of your life . . . that your life could mirror the hymn, "It Is Well with My Soul." Trust that your image of God could expand and keep expanding . . . that you could continually know divine love and acceptance in deeper ways.

Something practical you might do along these lines: search the internet for a list of God's names that indicate divine virtues and select a name to live with this day as you get to know the truth of God's identity found in that name. An example is "Emmanuel, God with Us." How will you allow and invite God to be with you during this day? How will you invite God as Emmanuel into every encounter, every thought? Reflect later today on how you experienced Emmanuel as present to you.

A MEASURE OF HAPPINESS

ONES HAVE THE OPPORTUNITY to let go of our hard-and-fast, life-denying ways of being in the world. We have wasted so much life on our rules and spent time measuring who's in and who's out—often just existing in a life constricted by rules of our own making that become the basis of living with resentment and discontent. There is a better way to live. The Serenity Prayer invites us to let go of our old ways of thinking and being, so that, like a cluttered closet that has been lovingly decluttered, we can make room in our hearts, minds, and spirits for the spacious resonance of happiness:

> So that I may be reasonably happy in this life
> And supremely happy with [God]
> Forever and ever in the next.
> Amen.

Singer and songwriter Bobby McFerrin popularized his lovely tune titled "Don't Worry Be Happy." I loved the song because it spoke to a longing I had to be really happy. Don't get me wrong—I have known happiness as a fleeting thing that had me smiling for a moment or two—but real happiness as a constant flow that I could access seemed elusive. A few years ago, I asked my husband if I could interview him. He knows me and so he didn't find my question odd at all. I pulled out my pad and a pen and I asked him, "Rudy, how can you be so happy?" I was poised, ready to write, pen in hand; I remember leaning forward in my chair. I knew that he knew something about being happy that had eluded me most of my life.

Without so much as a pause, Rudy responded that every morning he wakes up and asks God a question and also makes a request. "God, who are we going to help today? And let's have fun doing it." It felt as though I had just hit the lottery. I was so overwhelmed, pleasantly so, by his response. I understood the part about helping somebody because it's so much a part of our DNA as a couple and as pastors. But what sent shock waves through my soul was when he said, "And let's have fun doing it!" We Ones don't tend to prioritize fun. I had never once considered asking God for fun—that my doing, my very being, would be punctuated by fun. I guess I had not because I asked not. That word *fun* became my motto.

I am learning that fun is deeply connected to happiness for me. I am starting to ask for fun and to look for fun, and I believe it has increased my happiness quotient. I had no idea until that day I interviewed Rudy that I could ask God for fun—the thought had never crossed my mind. I tended to ask God for the serious stuff. So, as I see it, I am long overdue and I'm going to cash in on my happiness account by asking for more fun. I am willing to suspend all my old ways of thinking about fun so that I can "be reasonably happy in this life and supremely happy with [God] forever and ever in the next." Sounds to me like happiness takes practice, which I'm willing to start now!

Happiness is an intention we can set for ourselves. Seven and Nine friends on the Enneagram can help us learn how to relax and have more fun. Who are those fun-loving friends in your life? Consider an interview with them to find out their secret to happiness. Have you considered asking God to help you have fun as a pathway to being happy—to help you be open to an abundance of happiness? Do a thirty-day experiment and ask God how you can serve others and have fun at it. Try a new hobby or experience, even if you're not good at it (at first), just because it's fun—like my grown-up version of painting-by-numbers, a childhood favorite activity that I'm now loving again.

AWAKENING

THE SERENITY PRAYER OFFERS the One an invitation to awaken to the awareness that life offers us a fuller expression beyond our self-imposed limits and ridged practices. My hardest times in life have given me the opportunity—though in those moments, I couldn't name it as such—to stop and enter into my suffering to see what it had to offer me. I have always believed that life offers us lessons when we were ready. When I would be crushed under the weight of my self-governing, I learned to believe that God was present to me in the suffering.

Anyone who has experienced depression knows that it can create a sinkhole, with a daily falling sensation that feels like you're being undone. In my case, I learned that what was being undone was my belief that my "doing" was what validated my existence on the planet. That daily sinking into what felt like nothingness, called a pit by David in the Psalms, allowed me to let go of more and more of my notions about how I thought life should work and was supposed to be like. The more I fell, the less of me there seemed to be—the me who wanted to be seen as intelligent, well-organized, and industrious—but none of those attributes got me out of the darkness of the trial. The incessant falling day after day was a mental, emotional, and spiritual process that, one day out of nowhere, landed me at the feet of Jesus.

Looking back, I learned that I had to fall past all my notions of self and identity to realize that in and of myself I was not capable of sustaining my life. I indeed needed a power greater than myself to lift me out of the darkness and breathe life into me again. It had been a life of insanity to believe that I had to work hard to receive God's love—and I worked insanely hard.

What I learned was that each of life's trials, from the darkest to the lightest, allowed me to meet with God. Each time in the welcome, peaceful silence and stillness of recovery, comes awareness. I came to know more of God's love, compassion, and care for me. I grew to see that God wanted my happiness in life more than I had desired it for myself. I had taken myself and my world too seriously. God loved on me and helped me to laugh at the foolish way I had been using "try harder" as a means to access love. Though God's love was freely available the whole time, I had constricted it and tried to control its flow with my many rules and love-rejecting criteria of rightness.

Can you think of a time when you were awakened by a divine reality? How did you respond? How have you reflected on the experience to help you to stay awake? Try to articulate it: my most significant moment was . . .

What new awareness is grounding you now? Are you learning new ways of being? Are you releasing old ways of thinking that no longer serve you? Are you becoming more open to receiving God's love and acceptance, knowing that you don't have to work for or earn it?

IT'S NOT ABOUT
THE CHEESE

DURING THE QUARANTINE DAYS OF COVID-19, I succumbed to the doldrums of just getting the work done. I became inwardly obsessed with the clutter that my hubby and I accumulated during our "time out" together. Although I arose and prepared more days than not as for any workday, I was increasingly aware that these were not normal days. I noticed that little things that rarely bugged me in the past were bugging me now, and my old ways of ignoring my feelings began to creep toward the surface.

At one point, I almost banished my beloved to the hinterlands because he ate my cheese. I was fuming inside and knew that this grievous insult would have to be addressed—the sooner the better. I knew well the appropriate phrase from decades of therapy and married couples' retreats: "I felt blank (name the feeling) when you blank (describe the action)." But I didn't want to play by the rules—I wanted to have my say, my way. I felt as though my personhood had been attacked by my mate's confiscating and ingesting of my cheese!

I'm clear now that what I was feeling had little to do with my hubby eating my cheese, because I have since become aware that when situations are outside of my control, I need to look for what I can control. We Ones have to be honest with ourselves and those we love when we find our energies moving toward our unhealthy side. My beloved got a phone call that drew him away from me and the "scene of the crime," which gave me time to ask myself, *Why am I so angry?*

Thankfully, when I reflected later on the incident, I found that I needed to sit with the question and listen deeply. I used the "Judge-Your-Neighbor" worksheet from Byron Katie's thework.com and came to see that during the quarantine, I was working hard to make our time together life-giving for my extroverted husband. While I have worked from home for years, staying home 24-7 was new territory for him. I hadn't realized that all my extra effort to support him was causing me to desert my own self-care practices. Because I am an introvert, my need for silence and solitude were more real to me then than ever before. My unspoken expectations of how things should be—cleaned, stored, sorted, and the list goes on—emerged and I ignored it all those weeks until the cheese scene. For Ones, ignoring our feelings is life-draining.

One takeaway from my reflection was the reminder that I am responsible for my own joy. That is not a message that I gathered as a child; joy wasn't even on my radar. We Ones can become so doing-focused that we forget that joy is the marrow of a good life. The cheese was a fresh reminder that my default was not toward joy but rather first and foremost to the woulds, shoulds, and need-tos. For us Ones, it is essential to create some want-tos to make our lives rich and satisfying.

Another takeaway that I needed to reclaim was to allow joy to flow. I also needed to let go of being super hostess to my husband—he is not a guest, and this is our shared home and shared experience together. We were renegotiating under extremely unique conditions how we would be present to one another. His welcomed humor and easy smile were a gift, and just appreciating that anew had me already beginning to feel the joy trickle back in. I apologized to my husband for my response, and we reflected on our beautiful gifts of joy during quarantine . . . like sharing cheese and a lil' wine!

Ones can be stingy with ourselves, preferring to tend to others' comfort and support over our own until we bottom out and find ourselves empty. Start noticing what you are noticing. Are you aware when your emotional load is too much? Have you noticed when you find yourself frazzled, flatlined, or walking a fine line with family, friends, or colleagues? Have you considered renegotiating duties and tasks, or setting new limits as circumstances dictate?

Here's a practical way to kickstart the new you who takes responsibility for your own happiness: stand in front of a mirror, smile, and say, "I set healthy boundaries to guard my well-being!" until you can feel it as a loving insight, not a harsh criticism.

SELF-COMPASSION

SOME DAYS GET MOVING SO FAST that I hardly recall the details of one conversation, let alone whether I extended the courtesies of saying the magic words of *please* and *thank you*. I hope that I have been kind and generous with words that convey my heartfelt gratitude for acts of kindness and the like. We learned please and thank you in kindergarten, but how often have we allowed those words to fall by the wayside? I am reengaging these old standbys as a means of staying in the moment and as a tool for sowing seeds of generosity everywhere I engage with others, and I'm also training myself to love myself as well.

I am amazed that you can actually hear a person's tone change, even over the phone, when you offer the simplest thank you. We Ones are interesting, inspiring, and fair, and we can be compassionate to others, but we aren't necessarily kind to ourselves. So, really, I am turning up my pleases and thank yous to others for a selfish reason: to remind myself to be kind to me.

Jesus was being tested by the Pharisees when he said, "You shall love your neighbor as *yourself*" (Matthew 22:39 ESV, emphasis added). It takes practice to intentionally love myself. My little magic-word exercise is my way of practicing compassion toward others in hopes that it reminds me to cultivate compassion toward myself. I think it is helping. Sometimes I'll do something and just tell myself *Thank you, Juanita*, or *That was kind of you, Juanita*. I am offering myself the same compassion I offer others.

Recently I made a decision to take a self-care day, and once I made the decision, I audibly said, "Thank you, Juanita, I need this day of care." Is it weird to be audibly thanking myself? Sure—but I don't mind getting used to verbally loving myself well as an act of growth, development, and leaning to thrive. It's gotta be better than the self-criticism that flows way too often in us One types. Praise builds me up, and criticism breaks me down. Since I am the only person who accompanies me from the crib to the casket, I might as well build myself up—I have nothing to lose, and this is a test that I want to pass.

On a scale of one to ten, how would you rate your current state of loving, accepting, and approving of yourself? Of being kind to yourself? Of affirming yourself as an act of compassion? Remember to thank yourself when you perform random acts of kindness for yourself!

BE GRATEFUL

THE BEAUTY OF THE ENNEAGRAM is its invitation to know one's self and in so doing to know those areas that are prime for growth and transformation. I haven't known any personality tool as life-giving in its ability to invite me to be my best self. What I am finding is that life's invitation for transformation often comes through some level of suffering. Suffering can be the catalyst for significant spiritual metamorphosis; however, some simply seem to suffer with no apparent redeeming affects. But if one's attitude has any foundational quality, then gratitude is perhaps the best attitude for moving through suffering, accepting the gifts that suffering has been known to offer.

In *Disciplines of the Spirit*, Dr. Howard Thurman wrote, "Openings are made in a life by suffering that are not made in any other way. Serious questions are raised and primary answers come forth. Insights are reached concerning aspects of life that were hidden and obscure before the assault." In my own suffering I am often poised for finding the treasures, although perhaps not immediately when suffering is making the "assault" but instead sometime in the aftermath.

Gratitude helps to keep the soul open to being more expansive. The attitude of gratitude must be the baseline habit to cultivate long before the suffering arises. We can always choose our habits: bitter or better, ungrateful or grateful, desolation or consolation.

Gratitude is the energy frequency that is in harmony with the potential of possibility long after the experience of suffering has passed. Gratitude is expansive in nature and allows us to be open to the possibilities on the horizon rather than closed off and thus find our suffering in vain. We Ones enjoy exercising control, and the power we have in gratitude is the ability to take control of the direction of our thinking. I can choose whether my thoughts will spiral downward toward depression, shame, guilt, grief, or apathy. I can, in the present moment, choose gratitude and claim my power. Perhaps gratitude is the only power available at that time.

When Ones are thriving, we have the ability to stay openhearted, self-aware, uplifted, and inspired. These are true gifts of the thriving One. We can stay open to see through the lens of gratitude and opportunity; we can choose the habit of being grateful and continuously looking for something to be thankful for. Ones can shift and grow under stress and find ourselves living into a more expansive way of being when we choose gratitude as our attitude. It is in the expansive self that we connect more easily to the power and presence of the Divine available to us and loving us through our suffering.

In *Letter to My Daughter*, Dr. Maya Angelou recounts a time when she felt that she was going crazy. She called on her voice teacher, Wilkie, who insisted that she sit down with a yellow pad and ballpoint pen. Wilkie told her to write down her blessings—but Angelou didn't want to and told him so. He said, "Write down that I said write down and think of the millions of people all over the world who cannot hear a choir, or a symphony, or their own babies crying. Write down, I can hear—Thank God. Then write down that you can see this yellow pad, and think of the millions of people around the world who cannot see a waterfall, or flowers blooming, or their lover's face."

After engaging in this experience, Angelou concludes, "The ship of my life may or may not be sailing on calm and amiable seas. The challenging days of my existence may or may not be bright and promising. Stormy or sunny days, glorious or lonely nights, I maintain an attitude of gratitude. If I insist on being pessimistic, there is always tomorrow. Today I am blessed."

What are you especially grateful for today? Try writing out your blessings. You may discover a new habit of gratitude.

FREEING YOUR
CHILD WITHIN

AS A ONE, I OFTEN FORGET that Scripture says that "the joy of the LORD is your strength" (Nehemiah 8:10). In the second century, St. Irenaeus of Lyons wrote that "the glory of God" is humanity "fully alive."

Too often, I have operated as though joy is for other people. This serious approach to life has often meant the tragic loss of spontaneity, fun, and joy, which means that Ones often miss out on the sense of being fully alive.

Not long ago, my daddy said in a moment of reflection and regret, "I wish I had taught you girls how to play more." This statement caught me off-guard a bit. Both of us are hardworking, can-do girls, and I never imagined hearing my daddy say those words. I was so shocked that I didn't even ask what he meant, what he was feeling, or what he was seeing at age seventy-eight that he didn't see as a young dad.

I decided to call him one day and ask if he remembered saying this. Surprisingly, he said, "Very much so." His immediate response was, "People copy what they see. I copied what Momma and Daddy did—they were serious people and didn't play much. They didn't have much opportunity to play in a segregated Houston of their day." Daddy went on to say that he believed that as a means of safety, black church folks were often shunned from play, and so he copied what he saw. And I unknowingly have done the same.

Daddy said, "We need both the reward of doing good work and the joy and fun that comes from knowing how to play, to have relaxation, leisure, and recreation. We go, go, go because that's all we know, know, know!" Daddy also said we need harmony and balance so we can decompress from the stresses and pressures of life.

It is clear to me after speaking with Daddy that it is in the harmony of good solid work, relaxing, and liberating play—whether through hobbies, games, dancing, or other activities—that we are able to live fully alive. Joy is the marrow of a life fully alive; it is real strength supplied by our good and gracious Lord.

Does this story strike a chord in you? Has the responsible adult-in-you sacrificed the child-in-you and your equally important desire for joy, fun, and spontaneity? What would it be like for your adult person to allow your inner child new freedom? John Bradshaw has a wonderful meditation exercise called

"Embracing Your Lost Inner Child" in his book
Healing the Shame That Binds You where you go back
in time and reconnect with the child who got left
behind. Is it time to make peace with yourself, to make
amends, to be friends again, and to be there for yourself
going forward?

PRACTICE HAVING
A READY SMILE

ONES CAN TAKE THEMSELVES WAY TOO SERIOUSLY. I am grateful that I am learning the benefits of smiling. The body's chemical makeup is affected positively by a gesture as simple as a smile. A smile uses more muscles than a frown, and a smile releases God's feel-good chemicals of our biology. I hadn't realized the effect of my serious nature on my smile until life went seriously sideways for me. Only as I recovered from that bottoming out did I begin to relearn some of life's simplest but most important principles—like the power of smiling.

It had been my habit to listen to a local morning radio show as I drove the girls to school. The show starred a gifted comedian and his crew (they were conscious that children might be listening, so it always seemed relatively appropriate). One morning as we drove to school, the morning crew said something funny and I smiled. Afterward, my smile ached, and my mouth was actually sore from the smile because I was using muscles that I hadn't used for a long time. The trying experience from which I was recovering had not only robbed my family of their wife and mommy but had robbed me of my smile as well.

I was blown away by the physical discomfort that I felt after that morning smile, as though I had lifted ten-pound weights with my smile muscles. In that moment, I realized that I hadn't smiled in months, and I was totally shocked by the pain afterward—both physically and the awareness that my smile had been absent for so very long. Today, I intentionally smile to remind myself that I am grateful to be alive and I have another opportunity to lean into the optimism, the joy, and the wonder that being alive makes readily available to me.

My smile reminds me to lighten up and stop taking myself and this life so seriously, but it takes practice both for the smile and the thought. As Kirk Franklin sings in his song "I Smile": "I almost gave up, but a power that I can't explain fell from heaven like a shower. I smile, even though I hurt, see I smile, I know God is working so I smile." When I keep in mind that God *is* working, it reassures me that God is working all things for my good, and I might as well smile in honor of the good that is on its way. When I smile, I show that I am grateful to see the world as a safe and loving place, and that I am lovable and loved exactly as I am, because God said so. I smile.

Dr. Maya Angelou wrote in *Letter to My Daughter*: "If you have only one smile in you, give it to the people you love. Don't be surly at home, then go out in the street and start grinning 'Good morning' at total strangers." All change toward my growth and development require practice. I can practice on my face what I want to show up in my world. The more I practice smiling, the more I will find to smile about. Go out and practice your smile today.

NOTICING WHAT
YOU NEED

I AM AWARE THAT THE ENNEAGRAM has helped me to see that, when I am at my best, I can be dutiful, graceful, dignified, and poised . . . but when I am not at my best due to my neglect of self-care for soul, mind, and body, then I am skating on thin ice in my relationships. I have realized that when I am loving, nurturing, and kind to myself, then I am present to others out of a far more generous space. I have had to learn to be a more serene, unruffled me. I've had to learn what makes life rewarding, life-giving, spacious, and benevolent for me.

Howard Thurman wrote in *Disciplines of the Spirit*: "Growth means the experience of becoming aware of the self as self. Awareness of the self is rooted initially in the experience of the body. . . . To round out this experience is to take one of the primary steps in growth."

There was an extended time when I would push my mind, soul, and body to their limits because I was unaware of my own real needs. I had grown so accustomed to external cues for behavior that I had not cultivated self-awareness. Any feelings that I couldn't immediately compartmentalize got stuffed. Except for getting my hair done, self-care was almost null and void. I had no awareness of what foods were really nourishing for my body.

Even after bottoming out and then making some much-needed changes, I felt guarded and rigid around my needs being met. After all, I didn't want to relapse into the previous darkness. I know that I am an introvert, so I love when I've had nine hours of sleep to rejuvenate after being with a crowd. Because I know this and have decided to pay attention to my body's feedback, I now make no excuses when I give my own self permission to care rightly for myself.

This is a gift of the consciousness that is treasure out of the Enneagram, which provides knowing and naming as well as inviting self-exploration and awareness. I can name my gifts more readily, and then I can notice them and affirm them. I no longer have to burden my life partner or my friends, bosses, or children to affirm my gifts. When I'm present and I have cared for myself with sleep, healthy meals, fun, and adventure, then I am easily able to affirm my own knowledge with sheer joy and contentment. I become less needy of others and far more grateful.

When you are at your best, what do you notice about yourself? What gifts have you identified as yours to claim? What tools have empowered you to be your best you?

Sometimes imagining the new you is an important step to becoming the new you. Can you see yourself as affirming of and supporting yourself? Loving and approving of yourself? Noticing your limits and caring for yourself?

GROWING FREER, FULLER IN THE SPIRIT

THE GROWTH FOR ONES is to allow the Spirit who breathes within us to have fuller, freer, and more expansive expression. The Spirit longs to move us past our self-imposed margins with our sometimes low level energies of striving, rule following, and grinding. Our opportunity for transformation is in being willing to be liberated from our often narrow, restrictive, and rigid ways of being in the world. Self-deprecating thoughts of shame, guilt, and fear minimize the creative possibilities that are available to us all.

Consider the times when you weren't quite your best self emotionally and you got a call or email from a friend offering to do something with or for you, or they texted you a crazy joke. Your energy shifted upward. Your frown became a smile, and you were feeling light and joyful. These upticks in our energy are the Holy Spirit working within us. If we are mindful, we can recognize when God is sending people across our paths with positive messages in many forms.

We can choose to be intentional about staying open, setting the stage for the Spirit's presence in us. We can practice by saying every morning, "I willingly allow the Spirit to have fuller, freer, and more expansive expression in me." When we are conscious of the desire that God wants to be represented in the world through us as Ones, we can choose to stay open to the more expansive thought patterns, creative ideas, and solutions that the Bible calls miracles.

Just like sending others across your path, God wants to be seen and has selected you with your unique story, your specific DNA, and your special way of being in the world. God wants to be seen as love in and through you. Are you willing to allow God to be seen in you? What might hinder that flow of God energy and awareness in you? How might full surrender be freeing to you? How will you proceed?

> Meditate on Mark 6:1-6. Jesus is teaching in his hometown, but those who knew him only as the carpenter's son refused to respect or accept him, even when he was performing miracles. As you ponder the message, do any words or phrases stand out for you? Have you ever felt powerless in the presence of the energy of people who knew you when? How does this story intersect with your life here and now? What insight is God offering to you? How will you proceed?

PARDON ME, BUT YOUR ONE IS SHOWING!

I ENJOYED SCHOOL AND WAS THE TEACHER'S PET. But in fifth and sixth grade I got the stuffins beat out of me. I was looking down my nose in judgment, and two girls in particular weren't having it. I didn't realize that my thoughts, and no doubt my actions, indicated to these classmates that they didn't measure up to my lace socks and patent leather shoes, my ironed dresses, and my freshly combed hair. I was prancing like a peacock, and they let me have it. I was a child, and I didn't know that I was a One. I just knew that they saw something in me that they didn't like, and they put their fists where my mouth was.

Years later as I reflected on this brutal encounter, I saw what those two girls saw. I had privilege and I had judgment. I was clueless—and perhaps that is the challenge of being a One, because we are often blind to the way others experience us. While we are busy judging others and slicing and dicing people by our often-unspoken rules, we don't have any care or concern for their reality, their backstory, or their humanity. I have often grieved for those two little girls. I never got to know them, their stories, or their pain, but I am certain there was more going on than I would have been able to stomach if I had known.

I wish that I had known something about empathy and compassion. I thought that I was a good little girl, nice and kind. But in that setting, I imagine that little Juanita was unaware of the poverty that some of my classmates were living in, unaware of their unstable home life, missing parent or parents, vulnerable housing, and food insufficiency. My family wasn't rich; we simply had a different reality. In retrospect, I know that they weren't fighting just me, but instead they were beating the hell out of the life they were living. These two little girls are nameless to me now, but they have given me one of my most valuable lessons about the impressions that I leave on others, and the way others experience me when my One is showing.

When I see my false self, it can be shocking to my nervous system. Equally shocking is the tender loving presence of God reassuring me that I alone am surprised and shocked. God has known me all along and has loved me and longed for me to learn to love myself, even while I am being made new. The "god" of my childhood, the one I had dreaded and feared would punish me, instead meets me as compassionate companion and helps show me the better way to be.

As I became willing to treat others with tenderness and respect, as I learned to be grateful for the many things that others have to teach me, and as I became willing to let go of judging myself and others, my eyes were opened to a much more beautiful, kind, and compassionate way of living as a child of God.

How does this writing intersect with your awareness of yourself as a child? How have you responded to being surprised by your false self or shadow side? How have you come to know God beyond old, perhaps limited, beliefs about God? How have you experienced grace or gratitude?

DID YOU HAVE FUN?

GROWING UP WITH A TOO-STRICT VIEW OF GOD leads to a constricted life filled with rules and consequences, judgment for self and others, and a lack of empathy and compassion. Especially for Ones who are prone to this kind of thinking, it takes intentional effort to find our way to fully embrace the God of unlimited mercy, grace, and love.

A God-soaked, God-delighted life is expansive in nature. It is a life that needs no hard-and-fast rules on bad versus good or wrong versus right, because it is a life that is bathed in relationship with God—it is a life of being. In many ways, it was never about the rules, because it's always been about that relationship, what that relationship is teaching us, and how relationship with the Divine has formed and is transforming us. I'm now aware that God is not keeping a scoreboard on my righteous wins and losses; rather, God is looking to see if I am open to my heart beating as one with God's heart.

Jesus says in John 5:19, "The Son can do nothing by himself; he can do only what he sees his Father doing." God, I long for that to be the testimony of my mouth and my life.

On a day when I was on the mend from a severe trial, I had a moment of clarity when the Spirit said to me, "You think that when you get to heaven that I'm going to ask you how many people you led to salvation? No, I'm going to ask you if you had any fun!" I almost freaked out when God said that to me. Once again, it was a reckoning with the real life into which God is always inviting us. Ones have a difficult time letting go of our old ways of being. At times, it's like God is trying to pry our hands off the old life to offer us the new, more expansive one.

I had to ask for clarity: "Okay God, so I realize that I have gotten you all wrong, no thanks to the 'church' and all the many ways that reinforced my notions of a punitive God who doesn't play around. What do you mean when you invite me to have fun?"

What came to my mind was the first miracle of Jesus when he turned water into wine at a wedding in Cana (see John 2:1-11). I thought about feasts and communal meals as a part of the way that individuals had fun; how the festivals and holidays mentioned in the Bible were a means for play, relaxation, and revelry; and how they gave people, often of little means, an imaginative way of being free: free from day-to-day bondage, real or imagined, and free from have-tos and should-dos. Instead they embraced want-tos and the joy those want-tos offered.

I sensed this word from the Spirit and the Word as God's way of inviting me to just have fun: to mix, mingle, laugh, and giggle as a joyful, childlike self. This, too, is a means of entering into the kingdom freely, openly, and with playful vitality for living. Play is God's way of inviting Ones into a more expansive sense of self and a greater awareness of the kingdom of God, where childlike hearts and merriment are welcomed.

Do a search of the word "joy" in Scripture and then make a plan to read a new verse on joy each day. Ponder and meditate on your daily joy verse as you go about your life and try to see everything through a lens of joy. Ask the Spirit to give you new insights and inspiration each day. Then prepare yourself for a richer, freer, happier, more caring, and more abundant life!

ABIDING GRACE

THE BEAUTY OF THE ENNEAGRAM is that it reminds me that I am human, skilled at operating out of inherited sin, with a natural inability to be patient or kind, or to share and be vulnerable, as Richard Rohr defines sin. Yet despite my beloved rules and desire for "rightness," one way I experience God's grace and presence is when I commit to doing my inner work of transformation. I am no longer lulled into the false notion that I am perfect as I am, but rather I get to see that God's grace is present as I am seeing my shadow side—my unreasonable, judgmental, and irrational side—and that God isn't seeing all of me for the first time. I may be awakening to aspects of myself that I haven't before seen and known, but God has seen and known all along and still longs to be in relationship with me beyond my self-importance or self-righteousness. God loves me and is moving me consistently toward being my better self, and I'm grateful for that. My behavior and beliefs may be a surprise to me, but they don't surprise God nor do they distance God from me.

I used to gloat over the fact that I didn't break the Ten Commandments, until I realized that I had missed the real nature of the commandments. For example, I murder when I engage in gossip or judgment about another person. I murder their good name; I murder their reputation. I had never seen that before, and that realization has helped me to learn that just as others are in process of becoming, I am also in process. That awareness has been given increasing traction in my life. I am not free from sin or my imperfect way of thinking and being, yet I am divinely loved. By God's grace, I'm being shown that sin abides in me but that God's grace is ever present, healing me toward my better nature.

Knowing that God is awakening me to a wiser, kinder, more loving way of being offers me hope, especially when I can be blindsided by my beliefs that I am perfect and the world around me is flawed. I am made aware that I am in a constant state of becoming and that there is sufficient grace for me and those around me who aren't doing it "my way."

Reread the last paragraph. When have you had a moment where God has awakened you toward transformation? When have you felt blindsided by your beliefs, judgments, or actions? Most recently, how have you experienced the grace of realizing that you are in process, in a state of becoming? How did that make you feel?

Here is something I found that helps me in this transformation process. As you go about your day, imagine yourself with the gift of empathy, the ability to step out of your life and see life through others' eyes. As you come across people, say things to yourself like, "Just like me, this person is doing the best they can. This person just wants to be loved. This person has heartaches, hurts, struggles, and trials. This person could use an encouraging word, a pat on the back, a smile, a quick hug." At the end of the day, reflect on how much less time you spent thinking about your own problems and how the intentional experience of empathetic caring affected you.

SAVOR THIS MOMENT

I AM LEARNING HOW TO SAVOR LIFE. The journey has been made so rich for me as I have come to know another way of being in the world. I've learned that it is difficult to savor life when you are busy striving. Because a One's compulsion is to fix things, people distract us from savoring all that is good and right in the world, both in others and in ourselves.

I have taken up the practice of drinking herbal tisanes, herbal tea. Now, do understand that I come from a long line of coffee drinkers, but caffeine and I are not friends. I was introduced to tea as a healthy hot beverage alternative after a particularly difficult period of my life. During the experience of an artful tea ceremony at the Museum of Fine Arts, Houston, with Dr. Alejandro Chaoul of the Mind, Body, Spirit Institute of the Jung Center and Chris McKann, co-founder of the Path of Tea, I learned that tea enjoyed well can be a spiritual practice.

The tea ceremony invites the practice of savoring what is, of being present, of slowing, and of engaging all the senses through the selection of the cup, the experience of the warm tea cup clasped in your palms, the inviting aroma, and seeing the color of the tea maturing as it steeps. It is noticing the relative silence of fellow tea drinkers—all of this before one has even tasted the tea. Tea reminds me to slow down and be present to the perfection of God all around me.

There is no rush when I savor my tea experience; there is no judgment. Here there is only presence, like noticing fruity notes of a new herbal blend, or recalling my first cup of African red-bush tea savored in a lovely inn while visiting Zimbabwe. When I am present to my tea, it is the most profound reminder that I can let go of my feverish attachments to how I think things ought to be or should be, and I can simply abide in the moment . . . restful, serene, and savoring the goodness and gratitude in the moment as I abide in God. Drinking tea has become my daily practice; it grounds me, reminding me to savor what is, to savor the present moment.

Genesis 28:16 says, "Surely the LORD is in this place, and I was not aware of it." If you want a way to start thinking in the moment, try this: notice what you are savoring in your life right now and try to articulate it out loud ("At the moment, I love to notice the flowers blooming, the birds singing," and so on). Make a daily practice of savoring the moment. Let go of judging and worry as you observe. Breathe as though you were breathing in the essence of that warm, aromatic cup of tea or coffee. Let your thoughts ascend in prayer to invite God's presence into your moment.

THE NECESSITY OF PLEASURE

PLEASURE COUNTS!

I like a daily plan or at least a rhythm for my day, and there is nothing more frustrating than having my plan interrupted by someone else's poor planning. I feel violated and often fume a bit, not quite tea kettle hot but warm to the touch. Pleasure doesn't always set an agenda and book an appointment, however, so learning to stay open to pleasure is a learning curve for me.

During a rough time in my life, a friend of mine called and asked, "Are you going to be home today?"

I replied yes, and then she said, "Good, I'm on my way over." Before I knew it, I was in her car headed to the beach in Galveston.

I never would have permitted myself that luxury, that kind of upheaval in my day, but I needed it desperately. Her spontaneity was a divine gift at a very low point in my life, and I will always be grateful for her adamant insistence that I get in the car. Our drive changed my scenery and allowed the breeze to flow through my clogged head.

She didn't talk much except on occasion, and her voice was filled with love and affirmation of both our friendship and our mutual love for the presence of God. We walked along the sea wall and felt the ocean breezes, smelled the salt in the air, and felt the sun on our skin. We ate a seafood meal at her favorite spot, and then we got in her car and drove the sixty minutes back to my home in Houston. The whole experience was transformative.

I have often discounted the need for pleasure over my need for performance and production, but thankfully, that day pleasure won out!

Blogger Jayne Thompson, editor for the personality type testing website Truity, wrote the following in an August 2019 post titled "3 Things Every Judger Secretly Has to Deal With":

> We Judgers get so caught up always having a time and a place for everything that we never actually have any free time. If we see a window, there's a fair chance we're going to organize something into it. It's hard for us to justify doing something just for pleasure because if we can't tick it off our to-do list, what's the point?

Does any of this resonate with you? As I described my trip to the beach, did you find yourself wishing you had such a friend to come and scoop you up out of your mess? Something I learned was that I can also scoop

myself up and take myself for a ride—however briefly—
perhaps just by treating myself to a cup of tea or sitting
in a park to relax. What pleasures are you denying
yourself without good reason? What will you do to help
yourself change that old mindset?

DISCOVERING THAT GOD PROVIDES

IN ORDER TO KEEP WORKING, Ones will skip lunch, breaks, parties, socials, and the movies with our kids, even though we promised them all week.

I remember planning a family movie night for the four of us to watch *The Legend of Bagger Vance*. I planned the evening, purchased the girls' favorite movie snacks, and had the popcorn all ready to go. What I had not counted on was that my sermon was incomplete at that late point in the week. So I told Rudy and the girls that I wouldn't be able to watch because I hadn't finished my sermon. The disappointment was written all over their faces, even Rudy's.

As I saw it, I simply had no choice but to back out of our plans. I returned to my study and sat at my desk, torn between the family and the sermon. But I settled in and knew I had a greater "call" to complete Sunday's message. As I reviewed the Scripture and the notes I had begun to pull together, the sermon laid flat on my heart and my desk. I clearly heard the Spirit say, "Go watch the movie." I actually said, "I can't, I haven't gotten far along enough on this sermon illustration and it needs just the right story." There I was, saying no to God and justifying why!

My rules include:

Do the hard thing first.

Work before play.

Follow the rules.

These rules all stood on my side to justify why I had to keep grinding on the sermon. Finally, the Spirit said again, a little more assertively yet with the still, small voice that never screams at me, "Go watch the movie, Juanita."

Reluctantly, I got up and sat with the crew on the sofa. Even though I had missed a bit of the movie, I really got into it, and there it was, right there in the movie—the perfect sermon illustration. I was mesmerized by God's grace in that moment. God longed for me to simply relax, hang out with my family, and have a pleasant evening watching a movie I had yearned to see. The movie had my sermon illustration laid out for me in brilliant Technicolor.

How often have I missed out on God's gifts because I overrode that still, small voice inviting me to do the fun thing, the pleasurable thing, the thing that would allow me to see the wonder of a God who provides? God allowed me to have the quality time with my family that we had all longed for and provided the much-needed sermon illustration I had been working to find. Even now, remembering that moment fills my heart with gratitude.

When was the last time you allowed pleasure to win out over rationale or your schedule? How have you been surprised by pleasure or a plan to hang out that gave you a two-for-one benefit, like the movie I watched that had the sermon illustration in it?

If you need a way to think about intentionally incorporating pleasure into your day, you might use an acronym such as PAW: Pleasure, Awe, and Wonder. You can create your own word so it works for you. The point is to create a new habit of engaging in something spontaneous with yourself, friends, family, or a colleague. This helps keep you open to new experiences, such as a new recipe, new music, or just the permission to not have an agenda. It will help you practice being in the joy of the moment and staying open to finding God in it.

LIGHTEN THYSELF UP!

LET'S FACE IT, WE ONES CAN take ourselves way too seriously. When I was a child, I tended to commandeer the protagonist of all the games and play that gave me the lead role as the adult in the scenario. I was the doctor and I made my sister the patient; I was the teacher, the lawyer, and the driver of our fire chief pedal car. Even then, I was obsessed with being in charge and in control. So, playing for me was about imitating what I thought it meant to be an adult.

Many years later in an adult family gathering including my parents and my sister, my father said that he was proud of us girls. He said if he had known we would turn out so well, he and Mommy would have had more kids, but that would have been a crap shoot. We laughed. He went on to say that if he had it to do all over again, he would have encouraged us to play more instead of being so serious. Daddy said that both my sister and I had solid work ethics, and we were both committed and loyal to our vocations and relationships, but he wished he had known to teach us the value of the lighter side of life. In that moment, I didn't think to ask him to expound on the point, but his tone and sincerity said it all: regret.

I carried the same regret into my parenting, and now I am more awakened to the need to counteract my ingrained work orientation, the necessity of play, and the cultivation of imagination and the gifts they offer our lives such as awe, wonder, amazement, laughter, and lightheartedness. I have taken life way too seriously and have missed out on the spontaneity and the creativity of playing. As the old saying goes, "All work and no play makes Johnny a dull boy." Research shows that play reduces stress hormones and contributes to overall well-being. I recall a friend saying to my husband during a particularly difficult time in our lives that we needed recreation. Our friend said that in recreation we get to re-create ourselves, our energy, and our passion for living. I had never heard it explained that way.

I think that's why now I'm giving myself permission to take breaks from my fixed routine and play as an adult. Each of us has to come up with our own way of playing for fun and relaxation. When I reflect on what kind of play I enjoyed as a kid, the answer is usually something outdoors—so I'm recapturing the fun of the outdoors by hiking several mountains, riding my bike, sky diving, hot air ballooning, and getting scuba certified. These are some of the ways I'm learning to balance work with play. Another is that I have crowned myself as play buddy to my grandson. I've matured a bit now, so when we play, it's not my way—I let him lead. I know now it's not about winning or losing but that I play the game.

A friend of mine has a candle from Abbey Press in St. Meinrad, Indiana, which is owned by a monastery, thus many of their products feature monks. This candle has a humorous-looking monk with the words, "Lighten Thyself Up!" You would think if anyone took themselves seriously, it would be monks and nuns. That they created such a product shows both a sense of humor and the awareness that even an austere lifestyle needs to be balanced with moments of joy and lightening up.

When you realize you are in a too-serious rut, what does your imagination try to lead you to do? Why not start giving yourself permission to "lighten thyself up"?

FREEDOM

IF WE ARE FORTUNATE, we will die a thousand little deaths before we transition from this life to the next. We will let go of our old ways of thinking, seeing, and being that grew out of the quirky and sometimes dismal spaces of our imperfect childhood narratives. We will be allowed to see that our limiting beliefs no longer serve us as evolving adults. What freedom we will know when our thoughts become the mind of Christ in every matter. Freedom from dualistic thinking—this or that, black or white, good or bad, right or wrong—that makes no room for the differences of the creative other or any options between the extremes.

What a day it will be when we Ones no longer are ruled by our need to judge, discount, discard, or limit what fits into our narrow frames of reference and narrower still ways of seeing others in the world. Awakened from our foolish ways of living life, believing that we must master the procedures while missing the vital experience that is our life to live. If we are even more fortunate, we will be awakened by the Spirit of God to see ourselves as the beloved of God, wholly perfect spiritual beings having a human experience.

Imagine freedom from our egos, which are dictatorial, searching out for the familiar. Isn't it amazing that the last four letters of the word *familiar* spell *liar*? We will have freedom from the familiar constraints, bondages, and baggage that we have associated with our means of knowing security and control. In the Sermon on the Mount, Jesus tears down walls of nationalism, sexism, tribalism, and traditionalism.

The work of Jesus is the work of liberation and freedom. Any student of the Enneagram will see this Jesus model of liberation and freedom as we learn more about the wings and the arrows that affect a One. The wings and arrows provide means for growth, transformation, serenity, compassion, and point toward what it means to thrive as a One.

It has been by God's grace that I can see from time to time how I am being called into a fuller vision of my life, as God slowly and gently instructs me in ways that encourage me to a more expansive, more flexible, if not slightly scary, existence. But I'm good with what God is doing, and I have to say I've had such fun and joy since my crash, and I'm open to living my best life. So, this must be what freedom looks like!

Just as the book of Proverbs is a book of contrasts—the wise do this, but the foolish do that—so God has ways of helping us to see new things by contrasting them with old things. When we get tired enough of our unsatisfying, frustrating, even depressing old ways, God shows us what life can be like to be free of such things, to walk into new things, and to live life without being shackled to all those old things.

Jesus' coming to set the prisoners free wasn't referring only to physical prisons. What mental, emotional, or spiritual prisons have held you captive? Through Jesus, you already have been set free—you just need to step out of your cell and walk away a free person, a new creation!

TRANSFORMATION

THE MORE I LEARN, GROW, AND LIVE into my best self, the more that loving others urges me to relax, slow down, and not take life or myself so seriously. In my previous ways of thinking and being, I imagined that others were ill informed because they had no clue as to my workload, my goals, or, dare I say, the responsibility of "the anointing." The positive end result of crashing and burning was the freedom to hear new truths and write a new narrative for my life moving forward. I am so grateful for that fateful day. I never would have imagined that my life could be so life-giving, rich, and harmonious.

A sign hanging in my kitchen reads, "Never get so busy making a living that you forget to make a life," written by either Dolly Parton or that well-known writer, Anonymous. It's a simple sign written in white on my favorite color, orange. It is the kind of sign that you know you simply must have and it demands to be read routinely. It reminds me every day, in much the same way that the Enneagram acts as a memo from the universe, to let go of all thoughts of striving, busyness, trying harder, and all the stuff that I had imagined was the stuff of life.

My orange sign reminds me that memories are made when I watch movies with my family. When I say to my girls, "Let's go outside and play in the rain," it's okay. As some of these entries have articulated, in my old narrative I held life so close to the vest that I suffocated joy. Joy eluded me, and a bit of peace of mind required lots of aspirin and caffeine—and still it remained mostly elusive. I was trying to make a living and be a good wife, a good mother, and a good minister. I risked very little in the game of life, until I almost lost it all. Crashing hard was a long, slow wake-up call to a better way to live.

I'm determined now to *live* fully into the richness and expansiveness of life as promised in Scripture, the still moments with God as I quiet myself now that I have ears to hear, and the countless sources of joy, inspiration, and peace that surround me on all sides now that I have eyes to see them.

I am still not perfect, but now I know that I don't have to be. I am learning to relax after all, to not take my world or my life so seriously. I am taking lots of deep breaths and breathing myself into noticing what I'm noticing. I am so much more conscious of my thoughts and the kind of life that I really want to live. I want a life of happiness, well-being, and contentment, which means knowing when enough is enough. Knowing when I have worked enough and knowing when it's time to take a dance break or a laughter yoga break, or just a breathing break—a moment to simply catch my breath. The Enneagram has been a truly divine gift in helping me to have a kind of map for growth and awareness.

Today, I am a little more easily persuaded to relax and chill out, and I am a whole lot more open to cultivating happiness one moment at a time. I never knew the power of having happiness goals or joy-producing habits nor had I realized the countless magnificent benefits of letting go of the old me and taking God's hand to help me be the new me.

James 1:17 says, "Every good and perfect gift is from above." May you find all of the gifts that await you, just beyond the next prayer, the next decision, and the next moment of presence with God, who is the source of every good thing.

ENNEAGRAM
DAILY REFLECTIONS

SUZANNE STABILE,
SERIES EDITOR